Pádraig Pearse
and the
Eas~~ter Rising~~ 1916

Written by Rod Smith
and illustrated by Derry Dillon

Published 2016
Poolbeg Press Ltd

123 Grange Hill, Baldoyle
Dublin 13, Ireland

Text © Poolbeg Press Ltd 2016

A catalogue record for this book is available from the British Library.

ISBN 978 1 78199 888 5

Cover design and illustrations by Derry Dillon
Printed by GPS Colour Graphics Ltd, Alexander Road, Belfast BT6 9HP

This book belongs to

- -

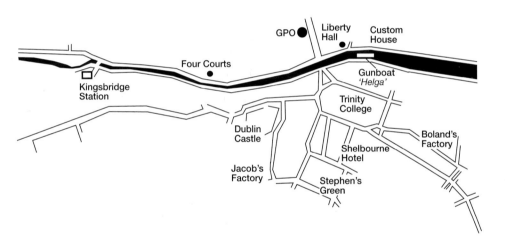

Available in the Nutshell Myths & Legends series

The Children of Lir

How Cúchulainn Got His Name

The Story of Saint Patrick

The Salmon of Knowledge

The Story of the Giant's Causeway

The Story of Newgrange

Granuaile – The Pirate Queen

Oisín and Tír na nÓg

The Story of Brian Boru

Deirdre of the Sorrows

Heroes of the Red Branch Knights

The Adventures of the Fianna

The Adventures of Maebh – The Warrior Queen

Diarmuid and Gráinne and the Vengeance of Fionn

Saint Brigid the Fearless

The Vikings in Ireland

Journey into the Unknown – The Story of Saint Brendan

The Story of Tara

Poolbeg are delighted to announce that some of our Nutshell titles are now available in Irish

Available now

Coming in March

It was a cold Easter Monday morning in 1916 when Pádraig Pearse and his brother Willie said goodbye to their mother Margaret on the steps of their family home.

"Yesterday you were the principal of St. Enda's school," she said. "Today you are the Commander-in-Chief of the Irish Volunteer forces."

Pádraig held her hands in his. "Ireland unfree will never be at peace, Mother. This is a battle I must fight." He gave her one last hug and a kiss.

Willie hugged his mother, saying, "Tell our sister we said goodbye."

Dressed in their green Volunteer uniforms, the brothers got on their bikes. Pádraig had a sword. He balanced it on the handlebars as they cycled away.

Margaret waved goodbye as they disappeared into the distance. "My brave boys! Will I ever see you again?" she wondered.

"Be careful nobody sees the guns hidden under your coat," Pádraig told Willie as they cycled towards O'Connell Street in Dublin city centre.

"Why did you choose the General Post Office as headquarters?" Willie said.

"It's a strong building, right in the heart of Dublin and it's the centre of communications. All post, phone calls and telegrams go through there." He smiled at his brother. "Dear Willie, we are cycling into the pages of history. Ireland will never be the same after this day."

Then Pádraig began to whistle and Willie joined in.

They arrived at the GPO where over two hundred people in the Irish Volunteer Army were waiting for them.

James Connolly, leader of the Irish Citizen Army, came over.

"Well, Pádraig, you've been a school-teacher, a barrister and a poet. Are you ready to lead a Volunteer Army today?" he said.

"Hello, James. Yes, I'm ready, but where are all of the other Volunteers? We were expecting thousands."

"A lot of people weren't sure if the rebellion was taking place. Orders were sent out yesterday by Eoin MacNeill to call off the rising. He believes we don't have enough weapons to fight." MacNeill was the Chief-of-Staff of the Irish Volunteers.

"But I cancelled those orders!" Pádraig declared.

"Yes, but people are confused. Anyway, I have my Irish Citizen Army who will serve under you, and we have the Volunteers who have turned up."

"What shall we do, Pádraig?" Willie asked.

"Today is our day, Willie. We fight! Go into the GPO and raise the Irish flags from the rooftop!" he ordered.

Within minutes, a tricolour flag and a green flag with the words 'Irish Republic' were raised.

"That looks impressive!" said a woman dressed in military uniform and wearing a feathered hat.

"Countess Markievicz!" Pádraig said. "It's good to see you here."

"This is a great day for Ireland," she said. "What orders do you have for me?"

"I want you to go to Saint Stephen's Green. Michael Mallin is in charge of the Volunteers there, but he needs a second-in-command."

"I am on my way!"

"Be careful, Countess. It will be dangerous."

"Don't you worry about me, Pádraig! I have my revolver. I am ready. Good luck to us all!" With that, the Countess marched away.

"The British soldiers who come up against the Countess don't stand a chance!" Pádraig said. "Tell me, James, do we have any reports on what is happening around Dublin at the moment?"

"We have Volunteer units ready in a number of locations. Éamon de Valera has just sent a message. He is in command at Boland's Mill and his people are ready."

"Send word to all units that the rebellion has started," ordered Pádraig. "We need to send messengers to the other Volunteers around the city to let them know what is happening. We should send food and drink as well. We don't know how long this will last."

James Connolly nodded. "We have a kitchen here in the GPO with plenty of food. I will get some Volunteers to see that it is done."

"Thank you, James. Now I think it's time to tell the people what is happening."

Pádraig stood on the steps of the GPO where a crowd had gathered and read a document that had been signed by the seven leaders of the Rising. This was called the Proclamation of the Irish Republic.

It declared that Ireland was now a free country, not ruled by Britain.

"Irishmen and Irishwomen, we declare the Irish Republic as a free country which is ruled by Irish people and not people from other countries. Every man and woman in this country is to be treated equally. All children are to be cherished equally. We promise to do our utmost to make sure everyone in the country is happy and prosperous. Thank you."

"Why are you doing this?" a voice in the crowd shouted. "Thousands of Irishmen are fighting a war against Germany in the British army right now!"

"We want to put an end to British rule in Ireland," Pádraig replied.

"You should be over in France helping to fight the war!" a man in the crowd shouted.

"Yes, at least you should have waited until after the war!" a woman yelled.

"We have waited long enough," said Pádraig. "One day you will understand why we have done this. You should be proud. We are the first country in the world to say that all men and women are equal."

A young Volunteer interrupted Pádraig to deliver a message. "We've captured some British soldiers. What do you want us to do with them?"

"Treat them in a friendly manner. Ask them to help with the washing-up in the kitchen."

"Yes, sir!" said the Volunteer. He saluted and ran back into the building.

Willie came running up. "The British troops are approaching! They're coming for us!"

"Well, we're ready for the fight!" said James Connolly.

"Get the men to stand at all of the windows," said Pádraig, "and tell them to smash the glass so that they're ready to use their guns. Fire the first shots over the heads of the soldiers as a warning. We want to avoid bloodshed if we can."

But the fighting began and lives began to be lost on both sides.

Pádraig sent units of Volunteers around the local streets to check all of the buildings. If anyone was found inside they were evacuated to a safe place, away from the fighting.

By Tuesday, Dublin City centre was getting pounded by the British army, helped by the gunboat *Helga* which had sailed up the Liffey. On Wednesday morning a rocket shell landed on the roof of the GPO, and part of the building went on fire. The Volunteers were able to put out the flames.

The Volunteers inside took turns sleeping on mattresses in corridors throughout the building, while the others kept a close eye on events unfolding outside.

Pádraig had some instructions for Willie. "Willie, at some point the British Army may succeed in completely setting the GPO on fire, so we need a plan of escape."

"If we go out on the street we'll be shot down."

"Yes – so take a team of Volunteers and start drilling a hole in the wall of one of the terraced houses in Moore Street nearby, so you can climb into the next house. Then drill another hole in the wall of that house and the next house after that – until you get to the end of the street. That means we can go from house to house, and get to the end of the street without being seen."

Willie went off with a number of Volunteers and did this. One of the houses they went into was a wax museum. Willie and some of the Volunteers put on the costumes of the wax figures and headed back to the Post Office in an effort to cheer everyone up. They brought some musical instruments back as well.

As the battles raged, the shops in the city centre were broken into and looted by the poor and not-so-poor of Dublin. Some people were starving and robbed shops for food. Others robbed clothes and sweet shops. One group even tried to rob a piano. Pádraig sent out some Volunteers to tell the people to stop, but there were just too many, and the looting continued.

By the end of the week about 2,500 rebels were fighting against about 17,000 British soldiers, much more than there were at the start.

By Friday, most places around O'Connell
Street had been badly damaged by the shelling.
The GPO and many other buildings were now
on fire. The heat was so intense that there
was only one thing to do: the Volunteers
inside had to leave the building.

"You have all fought bravely," Pádraig told them, "but it is now time for us to leave. It is too dangerous here. Please help James Connolly who has been shot. He has a wounded shoulder and a shattered ankle."

James was carried out on a stretcher. Pádraig was the last person to leave. He checked to make sure nobody was left behind. He escaped through a side street and entered a house in Moore Street. He walked safely through the holes that had been made in the walls of each house and finally came to the house where the Volunteers and leaders were resting.

Some of the Volunteers wanted to charge the British units which were now outside and in control of the streets.

Pádraig looked out the window. He saw an elderly man walking down the street. He was suddenly shot by a British sniper.

"Granddad! They have shot Granddad!" a young girl screamed.

Pádraig looked back at the Volunteers. "No more fighting," he said. "Too many people have died. This has to end."

Pádraig wrote a letter of surrender which was also signed by James Connolly. He asked his friend Nurse Elizabeth Farrell to deliver it to the British general. Elizabeth was a member of Cumann na mBan (The Women's Council) which played an important part in the effort to make Ireland a Republic.

Elizabeth delivered the letter and came
back for Pádraig. He left the house with her,
and met British General Lowe at the top of
Moore Street. He handed over his sword and
pistol as part of an unconditional surrender to
avoid further loss of life.

Elizabeth left to travel around Dublin, telling the Volunteers to give up the fight and hand over their guns.

All those Volunteers who were wounded were brought to hospital. The rest marched up O'Connell Street.

As they marched they shouted, "Are we downhearted?"

"No!" came the reply.

They laid their weapons down on the ground and were arrested. Some priests moved among them and collected written messages which they promised to pass on to their families.

The mother of a Volunteer arrived to check on her sons and was met by a British officer who knew her.

"I'm sorry, Mrs Kelly, that you had five sons involved in the rebellion," he said.

"I'm sorry that I didn't have five more sons to fight with them!" she replied.

Pádraig, Willie, James Connolly and the other leaders were sent to Kilmainham Gaol where they were sentenced to death by firing squad.

While in gaol, Pádraig wrote a letter and a poem to his mother.

"I have been hoping up to now it would be possible to see you again, but it does not seem possible," he wrote. *"I am happy, except for the great grief of parting from you. I have not words to tell you of my love for you and how my heart yearns to you all. I will call you in my heart at the last moment."*

When he was finished writing, he handed the pages over to the officer who was guarding him.

"Would you please give these to my mother?" he asked.

"You have my word that she will receive them," the officer replied.

The other leaders were also writing letters saying goodbye to their loved ones. One leader, Joseph Plunkett, married his fiancée Grace Gifford in the gaol eight hours before his execution.

In the early hours of the morning of May 3rd, 1916, Pádraig was led to the prison yard along with two other leaders, Thomas Clarke and Thomas MacDonagh.

The firing party was waiting, twelve men
with guns. Six men knelt on the ground. The
other six stood behind. Some guns had real
bullets, and some guns had dummy bullets,
so nobody would know who had fired the
fatal shots.

Each man was blindfolded. Hands were tied. A piece of paper was pinned over each man's heart. This was the target the soldiers were to aim for. Another soldier gave a silent signal to shoot. Twelve shots rang out. The three leaders fell to the ground.

A British officer sighed at the sight and said, "They were the cleanest and bravest lot of boys I have ever met. They died like lions."

After the executions, Pádraig's mother received the letter and the poem that had been written for her.

"There is still hope that Willie will be spared," a neighbour said.

"My heart wants to believe you, but I don't think that will be the case," she replied. "Anyway, Willie would never be happy to live without his brother."

She was right. Willie was shot a few days later.

The famous poet William Butler Yeats visited Margaret soon after.

"Most of the leaders of the Rising are all dead," he said. "Countess Markievicz was sentenced to death but was not shot because she is a woman. Poor James Connolly was not able to stand because of his injuries, so he was tied to a chair and shot."

"The Irish people will not accept this, Mr.
Yeats," said Margaret, tears in her eyes.

"You are right, Mrs. Pearse," the poet
replied. "Ireland will never be the same
again. All is changed, changed utterly. A
terrible beauty is born."

As news of the executions became widely known, the attitude changed towards Pádraig Pearse and the Irish Volunteers. People came to admire the heroism of these men. The British Prime Minister ordered that there should not be any more executions.

This order, along with the fact that he had been arrested later than the other leaders and was an American citizen helped to save Éamon de Valera's life. He later became Taoiseach and President of Ireland.

The remaining Volunteers who had been sent to prison were released much later.

The day of British rule was coming to an end. Ireland became a Free State in 1922 and a Republic in 1949.

In the poem Pádraig wrote for his mother before his death, he said:

"My two strong sons …
They shall be spoken of among their people,
The generations shall remember them."

Pádraig was right. Their names will never be forgotten.

The Wayfarer
by Padraic Pearse

The beauty of the world hath made me sad,
This beauty that will pass;
Sometimes my heart hath shaken with great joy
To see a leaping squirrel in a tree,
Or a red lady-bird upon a stalk,
Or little rabbits in a field at evening,
Lit by a slanting sun,
Or some green hill where shadows drifted by
Some quiet hill where mountainy man hath sown
And soon would reap; near to the gate of Heaven;
Or children with bare feet upon the sands
Of some ebbed sea, or playing on the streets
Of little towns in Connacht,
Things young and happy.
And then my heart hath told me:
These will pass,
Will pass and change, will die and be no more,
Things bright and green, things young and happy;
And I have gone upon my way
Sorrowful.

IRELAND'S BEST KNOWN STORIES IN A NUTSHELL

All you need to know about Ireland's best loved stories in a nutshell

Also available in the series

 The Story of Newgrange

 The Salmon of Knowledge

 The Story of Saint Patrick

 How Cúchulainn Got His Name

 The Children of Lir

 The Story of The Giant's Causeway

 Granuaile The Pirate Queen

 Oisín and Tir na nÓg

 The Story of Brian Boru

 Deirdre of the Sorrows

 Heroes of the Red Branch Knights

 The Adventures of the Fianna

 The Adventures of Maebh The Warrior Queen

 Diarmuid and Gráinne and the Vengeance of Fionn

 Saint Brigid the Fearless

 The Irish Vikings

 Journey into the Unknown The Story of Saint Brendan

 The Story of Tara

 ORDER ONLINE from poolbeg.com